**LITTLE GREEN
READERS**

# Our
# Plant Home

Focus: Habitats

Meredith Costain

We made a home
for plants.

We used:
an old fish tank with a lid,
potting soil,
little rocks and big rocks,
pieces of wood,
and small plants.

First, we put in little rocks
and put soil over the rocks.

Second, we put in big rocks and wood on top of the soil. We made holes in the soil for the plants.

Third, we put the plants in the soil and put more soil over the plant roots.

We gave the plants
some water.

Then we put on the lid.